AIR WAR
over
Southeast Asia

A Pictorial Record
Vol. 1 1962-1966

By Lou Drendel

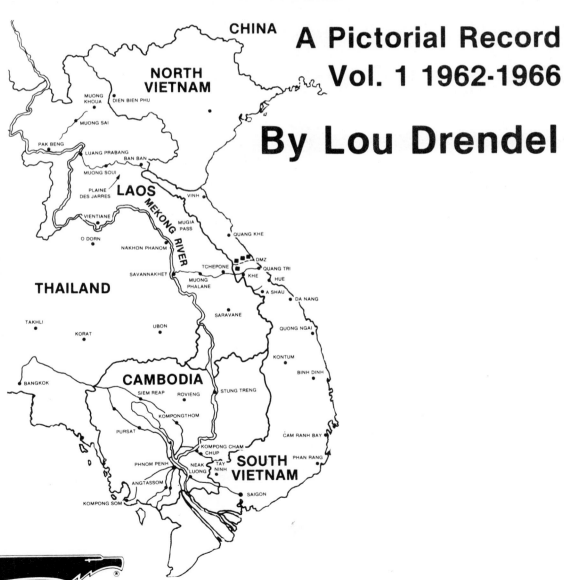

squadron/signal publications

The first American jet to drop bombs in anger against the Viet Cong was B-57B, serial number 53-3888, of the 13th Bomb Squadron, on February 19, 1965

If you have any photographs of the aircraft, armor, soldiers or ships of any nation, particularly wartime snapshots, why not share them with us and help make Squadron/Signal's books all the more interesting and complete in the future. Any photograph sent to us will be copied and the original returned. The donor will be fully credited for any photos used. Please send them to: Squadron/Signal Publications, Inc., 1115 Crowley Dr., Carrollton, TX 75006.

ISBN 0-89747-134-2

PHOTO CREDITS

U.S. Air Force
U.S. Army
U.S. Marine Corps
U.S. Navy
Norman E. Taylor
Paul Stevens
Charles B. Mayer
Sikorsky
Richard Copsey
Dave Graben
John Santucci
Republic Aviation
David Menard
Don Kutyna
Neal Schnieder
Bell Helicopter
Al Piccirillo

Foreword

It is now some years since South Vietnam ceased to exist as a political entity. As those final, agonizing days of April, 1975 recede from memory, it has become fashionable to refer to the Vietnam War as the war that we *lost*. That is a bitter choice of words, and one which is much too simplistic in view of the complex nature of our involvement in Indochina. Complex as the Vietnam War may have been, it was not unique in history, and the chronicles of war are filled with admonitions from some of the most famous warriors of the past which might have been written to fit our Vietnam experience.

The Vietnam War is often referred to as a "political war", with the implication that the motives for involvement were unusual, or that the rules for fighting it were different. Karl von Clausewitz, in his famous treatise *On War* said; *War is nothing more than the continuation of politics by other means.* The leadership on both sides of the Vietnam War understood this well. In the final analysis, it was their success....and failure....in rallying their respective constituencies to their policies that determined the outcome.

Sallust, the Roman Historian and Pro-Consul to Julius Ceasar, in his history of the Jurgurthine Wars, said; *It is always easy to begin a war, but very difficult to stop one, since its beginning and end are not under the control of the same man. Anyone, even a coward, can commence a war, but it can be brought to an end only with the consent of the victors.*

The foreign policy architects of the Johnson Administration might not have been students of Roman History, but they should hardly have failed to have noted these famous remarks by one of the greatest Americans of the Twentieth Century. General Douglas MacArthur, in an address to the American Legion in 1952, had said; *...and in the formulation of such policies, it is well that we understand that battles are not won by arms alone. There must exist above all else a spiritual impulse — a will to victory. This can only be if the soldier feels his sacrifice is to preserve the highest moral values. And we should understand that once war is forced upon us, there is no other alternative than to apply every available means to bring it to a swift end. War's very objective is victory — not prolonged indecision. In war, indeed, there can be no substitute for victory.*

Though our involvement in Vietnam was for the noblest of causes — to secure freedom for a nation that was threatened by a totalitarian state — the political commitment to that cause was poorly — and in some cases, less than completely honestly articulated. While Lyndon Johnson was promising the American people that he would never send American boys to fight the battles of Asian boys, (during the Presidential Election campaign of 1964) plans were being made to do just that. When American boys did begin to fight and die in Vietnam, it didn't take long for cynicism about the war to spread. An oft-repeated joke of 1965 went; "They told me if I voted for Goldwater, we would get into a war. They were right. I did, and we are!"

Archidamus III, the King of Sparta in the third century, B.C., said; *War cannot be put on a certain allowance.* Lyndon Johnson and Robert Mac-Namara presumed to know better. Ignoring the wisdom of the ancients, and the advice of contemporaries alike, they spent billions of dollars and thousands of lives on a gradual escalation of the war which only succeeded in convincing the enemy that we lacked the national will to use the full measure of our power.

Homer, in the Odyssey said; *It is not right to exult over slain men.* But when political equivocation denied the military the opportunity to end the war quickly, but still insisted on demonstrations of a gradual progress towards victory, the barbaric fraud of the body count became the scoreboard of the Vietnam war.

Cicero said; *The laws are silent in time of war.* But American lawmakers effectively ended the Vietnam War by cutting the feet out from under the South Vietnamese when they were facing their greatest challenge. By refusing aid during the final cataclysmic communist assault in the spring of 1975, the United States Congress made evident their willingness to abandon South Vietnam. The politics of the Vietnam War had been handled as shabbily at the end as they were at the beginning.

In these pictorial histories of the air war over Southeast Asia during the sixties and seventies, the people, the tactics, and the technology of that war will be emphasized. It will become evident that the fact that we *lost* the Vietnam War had little to do with our capacity to fight that war. Nor did we lose because of a lack of commitment by the troops, particularly in the early stages of the war, when President Kennedy's pledge to *bear any burden, meet any hardship, support any friend and oppose any foe to assure the survival and success of liberty* was still inspiration enough for those who would pay the ultimate price. It is my profound hope that these volumes will honor those who served honorably, for so little acclaim. But perhaps more importantly, they will help us to heed the words of George Santayana, who said; *Those who cannot remember the past are condemned to repeat it.*

The formation of SEATO led to many joint exercises during the 1950's, such as AIRLINK, which was held at Don Muang Air Base, Thailand in May of 1957. RNZAF Venoms were joined by USAF Super Sabres for this exercise. (USAF)

In April, 1962 the Marines committed a squadron of H-34D helicopters, augmented by O-1B observation aircraft and C-117D transports, to support the South Vietnamese armed forces. *Operation Shu Fly* aircraft and personnel were stationed on the former Japanese fighter strip at Soc Trang. (Sikorsky)

Introduction

The Vietnam War was the result of policies which were formulated during the latter stages of World War II. President Roosevelt, determined that prewar colonialism would not survive, opposed a French return to Indochina after the war. Winston Churchill, with a more pragmatic view of the post-war world, saw the French return to Indochina as both inevitable, (they had been there since the sixteenth century) and desirable. Churchill was not only the author of the euphemism *Iron Curtain,* he was also visionary enough to forsee it's existence once Russia had consolidated it's World War II conquests. He realized that the coming struggle with communism would know no boundaries, and that western influence in what would later come to be called the *Third World* would be essential to containment of communism.

The task of disarming the Japanese in Indochina after VJ day fell to the British and the Nationalist Chinese. With British sympathies firmly in favor of restoration of the French mandate in Indochina, and with Chinese indifference to anything except the traditional rewards of a conquering army, it was perhaps inevitable that their respective spheres of influence would bear the imprint of their occupation.

The allies had decided at Potsdam that the Chinese would be responsible for the area above the 16th parallel, while the British disarmed the Japanese in the south. The Chinese allowed the Viet Minh, under Ho Chi Minh, to consolidate their position as one of the most powerful political forces to emerge from the war. (The Viet Minh had proven themselves effective fighters against the Japanese and had received arms and advice from the American OSS during the war.) Meanwhile, in the south, the British disarmament force, which consisted of the veteran 20th Indian Division, under Major General Douglas Gracey, allowed the Japanese to keep their weapons and armed former French prisoners of the Japanese and used both in an effort to drive the communists from the South. French Gaullist troops returned to Vietnam in September of 1945, thus reinforcing a return to French Colonial Rule.

But in the North, the Nationalist Chinese were demonstrating the indifference to communism which would drive them from the mainland four years hence. Ho Chi Minh established the Democratic Republic of Vietnam, with Hanoi as it's capitol.

In 1946 the French recognized Ho's government, granting self rule to the Democratic Republic of Vietnam as a free state within the Indochinese Federation of the French Union. But they also declared South Vietnam a separate and independent republic, to be known as Cochin China. Ho Chi Minh was not satisfied with this, and late that year he launched surprise attacks on French bases which heralded the beginning of one of the longest and most costly wars in modern history.

In the early phases of this war, the superior French firepower prevented the Communists from gaining any significant victory. However, the Viet Minh military commander, Vo Nguyen Giap, subscribed completely to Mao Tse-tung's blueprint for revolution, and was satisfied to consolidate his position, while training his army and harrassing the French.

The communist takeover of China in 1949 was a tremendous boost to the cause of the Vietnamese communists, since it solved logistic problems and provided ready sanctuary. Giap was now ready to launch the more aggressive phases of Mao's blueprint. During late 1950, with much of the western allies' attention focused on Korea, Giap inflicted one costly defeat after another on the French, killing, wounding, or capturing some 60% of the French forces on Vietnam's northern border.

As a result of these disasters, the French appointed General Jean de Lattre de Tassigny as the High Commissioner of Vietnam, with sovereign power. This freedom of action, coupled with General de Lattre's understanding and use of modern firepower resulted in several impressive French victories during 1951 which forced Giap to once again retreat. The French victories of 1951 restored their morale and momentarily placated French politicians who were becoming increasingly war-weary. Unfortunately, the victories of 1951 faded with the see-saw battles of 1952, and the death of de Lattre, a victim of cancer, cast a pall on French expectations of a decisive defeat of the communists. de Lattre's successor, General Raoul Salan, received additional American aid in the form of M-26 light tanks, C-47's, artillery and trucks. What he needed most though, he didn't get. And that was manpower. The South Vietnamese Army suffered from an all-pervasive lack of enthusiasm, which manifested itself in desertions and a shortage of field leaders.

The French were spread paper-thin for a force that hoped to maintain control over all of the important population centers. By now, the Viet Minh were far superior numerically, and they were being supplied with more and more of the weaponry of modern warfare by their Russian and Chinese allies. There is evidence that theirs was not a popular movement, since there were

numerous isolated instances of resistance to the Viet Minh government. But for the most part, the Vietnamese rural population was unable to protect itself, and was forced to pay tribute and contribute men to the Communist army. The French, lacking both manpower and mobility, were unable to counter the Communist activities.

General Henri Navarre replaced Salan in May, 1953. His immediate reaction to the situation was a plea to the French Government for more troops and supplies. But the French Government was beset with increasing anti-war sentiment, fostered by the French Communist Party, which openly supported the Viet Minh. Navarre could manage no more than ten battalions of reinforcements. Despite this lack of support, Navarre decided that some decisive actions would have to be taken to slow the growing influence of the Viet Minh. In order to draw the bulk of communist forces into a set-piece battle, in which it was surmised that superior French firepower and air support would overwhelm Giap's forces, Navarre ordered the village of Dien Bien Phu, in far North Vietnam, to be taken by French paratroops. This action to follow the clearing of the Cochin Chinese coast between Hue and Quang Tri of communists by the South Vietnamese Army.

The latter action was a dismal failure, and probably denied enough significant support of the Dien Bien Phu operation to signal defeat even before it began. Nevertheless, three French Airborne battalions dropped into Dien Bien Phu in November 1953, and began preparing a defensive position. Giap took the bait and rose to the occasion. The siege of Dien Bien Phu was begun in January, 1954. It would be the last time that the French would underestimate Giap. By the time the decisive phase of the battle began, in March, the French had dug in a dozen battalions around the two airstrips they had built to provide supplies and limited air support. Against this French force of 16,000, Giap had arrayed an army of 50,000, which he was able to reinforce as his losses mounted. The numbers of the communist army did not surprise the French. It was, after all, what they wanted...a chance to get at the massed communist forces, and destroy them. What did surprise them was the fact that Giap had managed to manhandle heavy artillery through the jungle and into positions in the hills surrounding Dien Bien Phu. With these he was able to destroy the airstrips and many of the weaker French defensive positions.

The battle of Dien Bien Phu ended on May 7, 1954, as the French positions were overrun, and the remaining 11,000 survivors surrendered to Giap. Many of them subsequently succumbed to the brutality and poor medical treatment of the communist prison camps. The whole world had watched this battle, captivated by the romantic French practice of naming strong points after women, and by the bravery of the French defenders. It's loss was a devastating blow to western hopes of containing the spread of communism. It effectively ended the French presence in Vietnam, and weakened the allied bargaining position at the Geneva Conference which was convened that summer for the purpose of settling the Indochinese War.

As the French position at Dien Bien Phu had become more desperate, the American Secretary of State, John Foster Dulles, had advocated the use of American airpower in support of the French. He was backed in this position by the Navy and Air Force, but opposed by the Army. General Matthew Ridgeway had investigated the situation in Indochina and, realizing the problems an American Army would face, counseled against any involvement. President Eisenhower sought advice and consent from Congressional leaders, and when the former was negative and the latter was witheld, he decided against any intervention.

The Geneva Agreements of 1954, which were not signed by the United States or South Vietnam, partitioned Vietnam at the 17th parallel temporarily, and provided for national elections in 1956. It was expected that these elections would reunify the country under a government that was acceptable to the Vietnamese people. The government in the south was headed by Ngo Dinh Diem and was supported by the west. When the French left Vietnam,

HU1A takes off from the Royal Thai Army Artillery Center after a Combined Arms Exercise in July, 1962. It is armed with a pair of fixed, forward-firing .30 caliber machine guns and rocket tubes. (U.S. Army)

Bristol Freighter of the RNZAF at a Thai Air Base during 1962 SEATO exercise. (USAF)

Aerial reconnaissance over Southeast Asia was a hazardous mission from the early 1960s, when U.S. aircraft began regular recce runs to keep an eye on communist movements in Laos and Vietnam. This RF-101 was hit by ground fire over South Vietnam in 1962. (USAF)

they ended a colonial presence of over 300 years. Not the least of these was a large Catholic population, many of whom decided to flee to the south to escape the professed Godlessness of communism. An exchange of refugees between North and South consisted of 900,000 going south, while only 100,000 went north.

In the years following this partition, neither side distinguished itself with outstanding government. In the north, Ho Chi Minh's communist fervor resulted in thousands of land-owners being unjustly persecuted, with as many as 50,000 killed. This culminated in an uprising which was put down in late 1956, with the deaths of some 6,000 dissidents.

The problems of the south were greater in scope. Whereas Ho Chi Minh had one army, which he had formed and trained and which was loyal to him, Diem was faced with three rival armies in the south, **besides the Viet Minh!** In addition to the South Vietnamese Army, the religious sects of Hoa Hao and Cao Dai had armies of 15,000 and 30,000 men respectively. The Binh Xuyen army of 2,500 was considerably more dangerous because it was the army of the South Vietnamese underworld. The Binh Xuyen controlled narcotics, prostitution, gambling, and other traditional activities of organized crime in Saigon. With it's support, Diem was able to keep the Viet Minh out of his capitol city. Unfortunately, he decided that these groups would have to be eliminated or integrated into his army in order to maintain his control. His 1955 campaign against them succeeded in eliminating them as immediate threats to his rule, though it did drive many of them into the Viet Cong camp. Diem's rule became more autocratic with an obviously rigged referendum, in which 450,000 peasants cast 600,000 votes in favor of Diem, whose government was becoming more and more like that of his communist foe to the north.

Several B-26 and RB-26 Invaders were transferred to the South Vietnamese Air Force in 1961. B-26s were also among the aircraft types flown by *OPERATION FARM GATE* Air Commandos. These B-26s are seen at Bien Hoa, along with A-1s and T-28s of the VNAF. (USAF)

H-21 Shawnees of the 33rd Transportation Company (Lt Hel) were transported to the Port of Saigon by the USNS Croatan in September, 1962. (US Army)

O-1B Bird Dog in VNAF markings escorting *Shu Fly* Marine Helos on a mission in the Mekong delta in which the ARVN troops aboard the Marine Helos engaged the Viet Cong, May, 1962. (USAF)

ARVN Paratroops on a tailgate drop from a USAF C-130 during a practice combat operation in October, 1962. (USAF)

The Southeast Asia Treaty Organization, which had been formed in 1954, was made up of Thailand, Pakistan, France, Australia, United Kingdom, New Zealand, Phillipines, and the United States. Dulles had hoped SEATO would become the Asian version of NATO, committed to the defense of Laos, Cambodia, and South Vietnam. But the cultural and geographic differences were too great, and the United States quickly became the majority stockholder. Though Diem's excesses were distasteful to the United States, they were tolerated in the interest of protecting the south from the greater evil in the north. And Diem could be controlled to some extent with the carrot of American aid.

Support for Diem's government increased with the advent of full-scale guerrilla warfare in 1957. Cadres of North Vietnamese were regularly infiltrating the south, recruiting and training men for what would later become the Viet Cong. They used terrorism on a regular basis to embarrass the government. When Ho Chi Minh formally vowed to "liberate" the south, at a Party Congress in Hanoi in 1960, there could no longer be any doubt about the origins or intentions of the guerrillas in the south. The stage was set for a wider American involvement in Vietnam.

Captain Huyen Quan Trung, Executive Officer of the III Corps Signal Battalion, ARVN, and Crew Chief Sp4 Lundesgaard of the 33rd LTrans Co. check the action in War Zone "D" from a CH-21 in January, 1963. During the Battle of Ap Bac, five CH-21s were lost and 65 ARVNs with 3 American Advisors were killed in a clash with the 514th Viet Cong Battalion. This battle focused a great deal of criticism on the ineptitude of the South Vietnamese Army. (US Army)

1960-1966

While the Geneva Agreements of 1954 had guaranteed neutrality for Laos and Cambodia, the North Vietnamese never honored that neutrality. The prime infiltration routes to the south ran through Laos and Cambodia, and Ho Chi Minh was determined to keep them intact. During the late fifties and early sixties, both sides supported opposing Laotion factions in a see-saw battle for control of the largely agrarian country. The Geneva Conference of 1961 reaffirmed the neutrality of Laos, but changed very little in the eyes of the North Vietnamese.

In the meantime, the situation in South Vietnam had deteriorated to a dangerous level. It had become evident that it would require some American Combat Troops to ensure the continued existence of South Vietnam. American Special Forces were sent to Vietnam in late 1961, to act in an advisory role, but no one doubted that they would become involved in combat situations. That decision was reinforced by the on the scene appraisal of Walt Rostow and Maxwell Taylor later that year, and the first official Air Force units were deployed under *Operation Farm Gate* in 1962. This unit was dubbed Jungle Jim. It was the Air Force equivalent of the Army Special Forces...those darlings of the media, who had so prospered under the stewardship of President Kennedy. But Jungle Jim, aka Air Commandos, were ill-equipped to fight a modern army. They were flying the same aircraft the French had flown eight years previously...T-28s and B-26s, now resurrected as COIN (Counterinsurgency) aircraft. Also deployed to South Vietnam were 33 H-21 Shawnee Helicopters and 400 pilots and crew from the U.S. Army to fly missions in support of the ARVN (Army of the Republic of Vietnam).

In 1962 the North Vietnamese attacked Laos, prompting President Kennedy to activate one of the CINCPAC contingency plans for Southeast Asia. Joint Task Force 116, mainly air units, and it's deployment to Thailand in 1962 gave the North Vietnamese some cause to lower their profile in Laos. The Geneva Agreements which were signed in 1962 may have reaffirmed Laotion and Cambodian neutrality, and forced the United States (which did not sign them, but agreed to observe their tenets) to stand back and hope for the best, but they were little more than a propaganda tool for the communists. As early as that year, some American military men were calling for air strikes against North Vietnam as a way to cool Ho's conquestatorial ardor. The only alternative to this was the deployment of large numbers of American troops to South Vietnam, and everyone (well, almost everyone) agreed that that would be a mistake.

What the American President and his advisors chose to ignore throughout much of the early stages of the Vietnam War was the fact that, in the North Vietnamese Army, they were faced with a formidable, large unit army, capable of defeating a western army on their own turf. Counterinsurgency was popular. The *Ugly American* was a best-selling book, and it was fashionable to think of the communist menace as a covert threat. The American Special Forces could not do the South Vietnamese' fighting, and the Air Commandos, though doing most of their training from the front seat, could not win the war with their World War II vintage airplanes. Quite obviously, the South Vietnamese needed a lot of help. But there was a large obstacle to overcome.

President Ngo Dinh Diem had become his own worst enemy. The old maxim about absolute power corrupting absolutely was working overtime in Saigon. Diem restrained his more ambitious military leaders, fearing that their successes might make them popular enough to challenge his presidency. He persecuted the Buddhists, who played the American Press like a six string violin. Pictures of burning bonzes, coupled with increasingly frequent reports of inadequate performances of the South Vietnamese Army began to fill American Newspapers in 1963. Public sentiment was running strongly against support of Diem's regime. Clearly, something had to be done.

UH-1B of the UTT Helicopter Company, out of Tan Son Nhut Air Base, enroute to support the 33rd Transportation Company during a lift of ARVN troops during operations near Thu Dau Mot, 30 miles north of Saigon, February, 1963. (US Army)

Loading rockets aboard a "Huey Hog", one of the early gunships, in 1964. During this early phase of the war, the U.S. Army developed what were known as *Eagle Flights,* consisting of five armed Hueys, (one of which was the Command and Control ship, carrying the U.S. and Vietnamese on-site commanders) and seven troop carriers. The concept of the *Eagle Flights* was envisioned as a rapid-reaction tactical strike force, with a minimum of planning required for their utilization. By 1964 most helicopter companys had designated *Eagle Flights* on alert status. The *Eagle Flights* were among the most successful examples of joint U.S. - ARVN operations. (U.S. Army)

With the increasing Viet Cong activity of 1963, the large, highly visible markings disappeared from H-21 helicopters, and their gloss olive drab paint was considerably dulled. (U.S. Army)

A brace of H-21s from the 57th Trans Co (Lt. Hel) enroute from Can Tho airstrip to the landing zone of Ap Truang Hoa, 80 miles southwest of Saigon. They took part in a sweeping exercise against the VC in March, 1963. (U.S. Army)

Finally, it was the South Vietnamese military that acted. Several Generals approached United States Ambassador Henry Cabot Lodge, inquiring what the American reaction to a coup might be. Lodge, who had only recently been appointed Ambassador, and had seen Diem at his worst, relayed the General's concerns to Washington with a recommendation that we let the chips fall where they might. General Paul Harkins, head of MACV, and a man who had seen Diem under a better light, wanted to discourage the coup. Political pressures on the home front prevailed, and Lodge was instructed to let the Generals know that the United States would support any government that could hold the loyalty of the South Vietnamese people and fight the communists. The die was cast. On November 1, 1963 the Generals acted, surrounding the Presidential Palace, and demanding the surrender of the brothers Ngo. Though they fled through a secret passage, Diem and his brother were later captured and killed, beginning a parade of governments which only ended when the American presence in Vietnam was so widespread that some semblance of the electoral process had to be instituted in order to maintain American public support for the war.

PACAF C-130A in the 1963 markings common to the type. (Richard Copsey)

VNAF T-28D at Ton Son Nhut, February, 1964. With the promotion of Nguyen Cao Ky to command the VNAF, such morale-raising practices as the application of individual unit insignia began to appear on VNAF aircraft. (USAF)

"Jungle Jim" T-28, with U.S. "Advisor" in the front cockpit, and VNAF pilot in the rear escorting the aircraft carrying U.S. Secretary of the Air Force Eugene Zuckert on his fact-finding tour of South Vietnam. (USAF)

VNAF C-47 at Tan Son Nhut in 1964. This was the personal aircraft of General Vin Loch, Commander of II Corps. Insignias are carried on all four wing positions. (USAF)

The government which replaced Diem's was headed by General Duong Van Minh. (Who, because of his uncharacteristic size, for a Vietnamese, was promptly tagged "Big Minh"). Despite his imposing personal presence, Big Minh was a relatively weak leader. When Diem was overthrown, the communists correctly surmised that the resultant changes in all levels of the South Vietnamese government would present an unparalleled opportunity to gain ground in the South. Their offensive resulted in the eventual control of almost 40% of the South. Big Minh's rivals in the South Vietnamese military overthrew him within three months. His replacement was General Nguyen Khanh, who was much more politically astute, if no more effective in eliminating the communist influence in the South.

During a March, 1964 fact-finding tour of South Vietnam, then Secretary of Defense Robert McNamara recognized the danger of an imminent collapse of the South and recommended that U.S. aid be dramatically increased. The Quid Pro Quo was an institution of national mobilization in South Vietnam. Both American and South Vietnamese Presidents agreed to this, and American aid to South Vietnam increased from 197 million dollars in 1963, to 620 million by 1966. But money alone could not win any sudden reversal of the long and well orchestrated communist campaign against the South. The United States had arrived at the same crossroads it faced during the battle of Dien Bien Phu. This time it was not the French who would need help to defeat the communists. It was the South Vietnamese, and that made all the difference in the minds of the American leaders who were faced with another Vietnamese crisis. It was not a colonial army's chesnuts we would be pulling from the fire...it was those gallant, (if somewhat incompetent) natives of the South, who only wanted freedom and self-determination.

A complicating factor in the decision process was the American election campaign of 1964. President Johnson was being urged by his South Vietnamese counterpart to begin a bombing campaign against the north. Johnson's opponent in the election, Barry Goldwater, advocated a tougher line in American Vietnam policy. President Johnson, though, was more interested in fighting his war on poverty, and while he was more than willing to throw money into Indochina, he was not willing to risk the possible political ramifications of decisive action. In fact, throughout the campaigning, Johnson repeatedly pledged that he would not *send American Boys to fight the battles of Asian Boys,* while his campaign publicists portrayed Goldwater as an irresponsible military adventurist.

Johnson's dilemma (if it could be characterised as such) was solved by the North Vietnamese. While there was little concrete proof that the North was promulgating the war in the South, conducting a full-scale bombing campaign against North Vietnam would have been a risky political venture. When U.S. destroyers, which had been sailing on international waters in the Gulf of Tonkin, were attacked by North Vietnamese torpedo boats on August 2 and 4, 1964, LBJ was able to extract the maximum political mileage from what came to be know as the *Tonkin Gulf Incident.* The destroyers had been engaged in *Desoto Patrols* which were intelligence gathering missions, and the North Vietnamese could hardly have been faulted for thinking that they could get away with attacking them, since all of South Vietnam was on the brink of falling to the North, and the U.S. had offered little more than token resistance.

Military Air Transport Service (MATS) C-135 at Tan Son Nhut airport in 1964, during the beginning of the massive airlift of supplies to South Vietnam. (USAF)

Beech U-8 at Tan Son Nhut, February 1964.

C-123 at Tan Son Nhut, 1964. The Provider provided much of the airlift capability of USAF early in the war. (USAF)

(Above) The first jet aircraft to be introduced to the war zone was the B-57 Canberra. B-57s of the 8th and 13th Bomb Squadrons arrived at Bien Hoa in August, 1964. (USAF)

In an effort to impress the Viet Cong with our resolve, the B-57s flew regular training missions at relatively low levels over the Mekong Delta during 1964. Some of these missions were designated as road reconnaissance, but the Canberras were unarmed. (USAF)

What the North Vietnamese did not know was that the American leadership was well aware of the seriousness of the situation, and was only waiting for the opportunity to extend it's involvement. The Joint Chiefs of Staff had ordered a list of strategic targets be drawn up by the Defense Intelligence Agency (DIA). The DIA came up with a list of 94 of the most critical war-making targets in North Vietnam, and the Air Staff developed a coordinated aerial campaign to destroy them in the quickest way possible. President Johnson did not consider the attacks on the Destroyers Maddox and Turner Joy sufficient provocation for all out attacks. But he did use the power of the Presidency to authorize retaliatory strikes on the bases of the torpedo boats and the oil storage facilities at Vinh. The U.S. Congress apparently agreed wholeheartedly with his actions, for they gave almost unanimous approval to the Tonkin Gulf Resolution, which authorized the President to *take all necessary steps including the use of armed force to assist any member or protocol state of the Southeast Asia Treaty Organization.* In effect, congress had transferred their war-making decision to the President. Johnson, with one eye on the election, was unwilling to authorize the all out attacks which were

a part of the JCS plan for the 94 target list, and which the American Ambassador to South Vietnam, Maxwell Taylor was urging.

The American attacks on the North Vietnamese bases had the opposite effect from that desired or expected by the President and his advisors. Far from discouraging Ho, these attacks injected new vigor into his campaign of subversion in the South. The situation in South Vietnam was becoming more tenuous by the day, and General Khanh was repeating many of Diem's mistakes in his efforts to consolidate his power. The communists had good reason to believe that they were on the threshold of victory in the south, and the attacks on the torpedo boat bases were little more than nuisance raids, which only served to increase the flow of air defense weaponry from Russia and China. Two days before the American election, the Viet Cong attacked Bien Hoa Air Base, north of Saigon, destroying six B-57's, killing five and wounding 76 Americans. This was a provocation much more serious than the ineffectual torpedo boat attacks, but Ambassador Taylor's plea for a concerted attack on North Vietnam in response to the Bien Hoa attack was again ignored in Washington.

(Left) When the sight and sound of the B-57 failed to deter the Viet Cong, the 8th and 13th BSs started flying missions for real. The first bombs dropped from a jet in the Vietnam War were delivered by B-57B, 53-3888 of the 13th BS on 19 February, 1965. (USAF)

(Middle) B-57s were equipped with black powder cartridge starting systems, which allowed them to operate from strips without the use of APUs. (USAF)

(Bottom) Checking the bomb load in the rotary bomb bay of the B-57 prior to takeoff. (USAF)

13

(Above Left) Captain Enos Chabot checks 500LB "slick" bombs on his preflight. Mission was flown by the 8th BS from Bien Hoa, and was O-1 FAC-controlled, March, 1965. (Left) B-57 taxies out for a mission from Danang, December, 1965. The B-57s were moved from Bien Hoa, to Tan Son Nhut, and finally to Danang, in June. They were used in a variety of missions, from flak-supression for the C-123 *Ranch Hand* defoliation aircraft, to night interdiction missions against North Vietnam. It was these missions that inspired the *DOOM PUSSY, DOOM* stood for Danang Officer's Open Mess. The *O* club at Danang in the best World War II traditions, had a wooden carved cat on the back of the bar, which was turned face to the back wall when crews were up north on these missions. (Below) The B-57 could carry 5,000LBS of bombs in the rotary bay, and 3,000LBS on four wing stations. They also carried 20MM cannon in the wings. (Note stains from muzzle gases underwings). The impressive bomb load of the B-57 made it an effective close air support aircraft, and it was the first jet aircraft the VNAF flew. VNAF had four B-57s, but the program faltered, and with the accidental death of Major N.N. Bien, one of the prime-movers of the VNAF B-57 operation, it was terminated in late 1966. (All photos USAF)

UH-1B of the 145th Airlift Platoon enroute from the Mekong Delta to Saigon, 10 December 1964. General Harold K. Johnson, Army Chief of Staff was aboard, having just completed an inspection of ARVN units in the Delta. (U.S. Army)

As the situation in South Vietnam deteriorated throughout 1964, it became necessary to provide additional American airpower. These F-102s flew combat air patrols against the possibility of the North Vietnamese sending their IL-28 light bombers south. (USAF)

Though President Johnson won an overwhelming victory at the polls in 1964, a Harris poll showed that little more than half the people who voted for him approved of his handling of the Vietnam situation. (It is safe to assume that a much greater majority of the people who did not vote for him disapproved of his handling of the war.) It should have been clear from this sampling of opinion that some sort of decisive action was what the American People wanted, but Washington continued to vacillate.

Instead of the concerted attack on the 94 target list, which the Joint Chiefs of Staff (JCS) went on record in favor of after the Bien Hoa attack, Johnson opted for a graduated response, beginning with the attacks on targets just above the DMZ and working northward if the North Vietnamese continued their attacks against our bases and personnel in the south. LBJ, the political animal, sure that every man had his price, determined to turn the screws on the North Vietnamese until they were in an accomodating mood. Unfortunately, the North Vietnamese expectations of what the United States would do next was always more severe than what President Johnson was willing to authorize. *Operation Barrel Roll,* begun in December, 1964 against the Ho Chi Minh Trail in Laos consisted of two weekly flights of four aircraft each. This was a laughably small force to be throwing against the major infiltration route to the south...a route which thousands of men and incalculable amounts of war material were using. The North Vietnamese, far from being terrorized by this aerial campaign, did not even realize that it had begun!

There were deep divisions within the Johnson administration on the use of airpower. The JCS believed that the most effective way to use our superior airpower was to destroy the North's war-making potential at it's source. Their list of 94 targets included ports and staging areas for war materiel, lines of communications within North Vietnam, and some of North Vietnam's industry. They argued that it would be far less costly, both in terms of lives and money, to destroy these supplies before they were dispersed to the south and in use against the U.S. and South Vietnamese. In addition to this, bombing the North's most heavily populated areas would bring home to the North Vietnamese people the consequences of their leader's policies in the south. Robert McNamara argued that since the war was being fought in the south, that was where we should concentrate our airpower, using it in a purely tactical sense, limiting strategic strikes to the Ho Chi Minh Trail. President Johnson, while mindful of the shock value a large strike against the 94 target list would have on the North Vietnamese, was also fearful that this might bring direct intervention from the Chinese.

Two of the larger workhorses in the USAF airlift effort during the early 1960s were the C-124 (background) and the C-133. Both were built by Douglas, but the turboprop 133 carried nearly twice the load over the same distance. Tan Son Nhut, February, 1964. (USAF)

30 RA-3Bs were built for the Navy by Douglas. The five man crew operated a variety of camera equipment to provide attack carriers with a great deal of their tactical reconnaissance capability. (U.S. Navy)

Loading Zuni rockets aboard an F-8 Crusader of VF-51 in the Gulf of Tonkin, August, 1964. F-8s from the Ticonderoga were among the aircraft which retaliated against North Vietnamese torpedo boat bases after the Tonkin Gulf Incident. (U.S. Navy)

In the meantime, the political situation in South Vietnam was deteriorating rapidly. General Khanh was unable to rally the South Vietnamese people to his government. The army was showing itself to be incompetent and ineffectual. Younger officers in the military pressured Khanh to step down, a move he would not make, though he did form several governments in an effort to placate first the military, then the Buddhists. Viet Cong attacks in the south were becoming more direct, more numerous, and more devastating. During a visit to South Vietnam by National Security Advisor McGeorge Bundy, the Viet Cong attacked an American base near Plieku, killing nine and wounding one hundred Americans. President Johnson was urged to retaliate with the full force of our airpower to this provocation. His response was *Flaming Dart*, a series of strikes against military barracks at Dong Hoi, just above the DMZ. Continued attacks by the Viet Cong led to the initiation of *Rolling Thunder*.

In spite of it's ominous name, *Rolling Thunder* was anything but the cataclysmic event needed to convince the North Vietnamese that their actions in the south would bring the war home to the north in spades. In fact, it could be convincingly argued that the timid manner in which this campaign began (mainly against targets below the 19th parallel, with few targets of any consequence released for destruction, and with strict rules of engagement against North Vietnamese air defenses) only served to harden the resolve of the communists, and allowed them ample time to build what was eventually conceded to be the toughest air defense system in the history of aerial warfare. President Johnson was now in the position of having what amounted to an adversary relationship with the military. The JCS, with a purely military view of the war, looked upon North Vietnam as a series of strategic targets. The President, still fearful that too much pressure on the north would bring in the Chinese, saw only limited tactical targets.

The Administration was far from unanimous in it's assesment of how the Vietnam situation should be handled. The military, of course, was inclined to swift and complete destruction of the source of the problem. That is, the war-making potential of the North Vietnamese. George Ball, a U.S. Undersecretary of State, was opposed to any military action, proposing negotiations as the only solution to the Southeast Asian problem. The majority of opinion in the State Department and the White House followed the recommendations of a paper on insurgency written by State Department counselor Walt Rostow. Rostow advocated a gradual escalation of pressures on the North Vietnamese, arguing that sooner or later the communists would feel that any possible Viet Cong victory was not worth the price they had to pay. It was a solution that appealed to Lyndon Johnson, the wheeler-dealer politician, for it allowed him maximum latitude to use all options in trying to strike a deal with the other side. In spite of the fact that the North Vietnamese time and again demonstrated that they would disdain any treaty or commitment as long as it was not enforced, this administration, and those that followed, continued to strive for a negotiated settlement to the war.

(Above) F-8E returning to Coral Sea after a combat mission over North Vietnam in March, 1965. F-8s and Skyhawks from Hancock and Coral Sea had just struck radar sites in the North. (U.S. Navy)

Positioning a Crusader on the catapult prior to a combat mission from CVA-19 Hancock at the beginning of *Rolling Thunder*, March, 1965. (U.S. Navy)

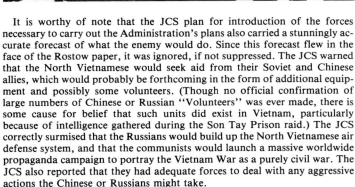

It is worthy of note that the JCS plan for introduction of the forces necessary to carry out the Administration's plans also carried a stunningly accurate forecast of what the enemy would do. Since this forecast flew in the face of the Rostow paper, it was ignored, if not suppressed. The JCS warned that the North Vietnamese would seek aid from their Soviet and Chinese allies, which would probably be forthcoming in the form of additional equipment and possibly some volunteers. (Though no official confirmation of large numbers of Chinese or Russian "Volunteers" was ever made, there is some cause for belief that such units did exist in Vietnam, particularly because of intelligence gathered during the Son Tay Prison raid.) The JCS correctly surmised that the Russians would build up the North Vietnamese air defense system, and that the communists would launch a massive worldwide propaganda campaign to portray the Vietnam War as a purely civil war. The JCS also reported that they had adequate forces to deal with any aggressive actions the Chinese or Russians might take.

Much has been made of the failure of U.S. Airpower to live up to it's vaunted reputation during the Vietnam War. This negative assessment might deceive those who were ignorant of the limitations under which airpower was employed. (If you believe that a majority of the national press was being honest in it's reportage of the air war, then you can only ascribe their obvious inaccuracies to ignorance.) It certainly did not fool communist strategists, though it may have puzzled them. It did fool much of the American electorate during most of the war.

The first American ground combat units to be introduced into Vietnam came ashore in March, 1965. The 9th Marine Expeditionary Brigade was assigned to protect the major U.S. airbase at Danang. This airfield security was deemed necessary, since many of the strikes against North Vietnam would originate from Danang. (The South Vietnamese had been providing airfield security, but it was felt that they would be better employed to go after

the Viet Cong in the bush.) Providing airfield security eventually became an active rather than passive mission, as the deficiencies of the South Vietnamese armed forces became more evident and the VC seemed able to roam the countryside at will. Marine airpower increased as the need to provide close air support for the Marine ground forces escalated.

The North Vietnamese continued to build their air defense systems and to step up their infiltration of the south throughout 1965. The first American aircraft to be shot down by a SAM was lost in July. The Migs had claimed their first victims in April. All of this activity was well documented, and the JCS continued to ask permission to strike the ever-expanding air defense network and to destroy the stockpiles of war material before it was dispersed to the infiltration routes. The Administration continued to look to South Vietnam as the battleground, and the buildup of U.S. ground combat forces gained momentum throughout 1965. But it had become painfully evident by the end of 1965 that the only initiative that the United States had was in the employment of it's airpower against North Vietnam. There, the North Vietnamese could only react to American actions. In the south, the NVA could attack at will, and retreat to Laotian or Cambodian sanctuaries whenever they wished. Following Mao's tenets, they only attacked when they had a clear and overwhelming advantage.

The civilian and military view of the war grew further apart daily. Whereas the military was forced to deal with the reality of on-scene threats, the people in Washington continued to believe that their limited war counterinsurgency plans would end the war.

This Crusader was hit by AAA and damaged beyond safe recovery aboard the Coral Sea. The pilot ejected safely shortly after this picture was taken, and was picked up by the Plane Guard Helo. (U.S. Navy)

The Xom Ca Trang bridge in North Vietnam was knocked down by Navy planes on April 16, 1965. A Bullpup Missile launched from one of the Coral Sea's Skyhawks made a direct hit on one of the center spans. (U.S. Navy)

An S-2 Tracker is positioned for launch from CVA-61, Ranger in March 1965. (U.S. Navy)

(Above) Crew members of CVA-43, Coral Sea, proclaiming their nearly year long stint in the Western Pacific in 1965, during which Air Wing 15 aircraft flew 160 strikes, delivering 6,000 tons of ordnance on the Communists. (U.S. Navy)

CVA-41 Midway and DD-877 Perkins are refuelled by AO-148 Ponchatoula, enroute to the Gulf of Tonkin in April, 1965. Air Wing Two was aboard Midway. (U.S. Navy)

USS Ticonderoga (CVA-14) answered the North Vietnamese Torpedo Boat attacks in August, 1964. Tico was also the first carrier to complete three combat cruises, and aircraft from her air group were the first to strike Haiphong. (U.S. Navy)

Skyhawks, Skyraiders, and Phantoms aboard the Coral Sea in January, 1965. In June the Skyraiders of VA-25 were destined to make one of only two Mig kills by the venerable Spad. (U.S. Navy)

Early in 1966, Secretary McNamara provided aid and comfort to the enemy by publicly stating that U.S. *objectives are not to destroy or to overthrow the Communist government of China or the Communist government of North Vietnam. They are limited to the destruction of the insurrection and aggression directed by North Vietnam against the political institutions of South Vietnam. This is a very, very limited political objective.* In the eyes of the North Vietnamese, this could only be reaffirmation of their contention that the U.S. was a paper tiger.

In spite of this message of reassurance to North Vietnam, more and more targets were released throughout 1966. Unfortunately, the key targets were still on the proscribed list. So, while what we hit was devastated, what we did not hit made more of an impression on the enemy. Some political leaders mistakenly thought that this was clear evidence of the inability of airpower to influence enemy thinking. The President may have believed that by gradually hitting targets of increasing importance he would get the North Vietnamese' allies used to the idea that we would not give in, and that they had little to gain by supporting a government so intransigent that it would not even negotiate a settlement. This may have been what he had in mind when he advocated *a great deal of patience* in dealing with the war during his State of the Union address in early 1967.

The air war in South Vietnam was under the direct control of Military Assistance Command, Vietnam. (MACV) and it's commander, General William C. Westmoreland. It had become clear to Westmoreland that South Vietnam was in real danger of falling before the end of 1965 if something drastic was not done to strenghten ARVN. It was obvious to him that the South Vietnamese army was incapable of holding it's own against regular units of the North Vietnamese Army, which had been spotted in the central highlands, poised to cut the country in half. The only alternative he could see was the introduction of more SEATO or American combat troops. This buildup began almost immediately. Since he did not want to risk demoralizing the South Vietnamese any more than they already were, he did not integrate their troops into his direct command structure. He hoped to foster independence and a sense of pride in their own abilities by maintaining this ''separate but equal'' policy. Unfortunately, it would have the opposite effect. But in 1965 and 1966 there was a sense that we could defeat the North Vietnamese on the battlefield in South Vietnam, then turn over a pacified countryside to ARVN while we withdrew.

(Above) USS Constellation (CVA-64) joined the Ticonderoga for retaliatory strikes against North Vietnamese PT boats. (U.S. Navy)

RF-8A of VFP-63 is readied for launch from Ranger (CVA-61). Ranger participated in *Flaming Dart I,* the strikes ordered after Viet Cong attacks on American Bases in South Vietnam in February, 1965. This RF-8 is about to be launched to provide post-strike battle damage assessment photos from that strike. (U.S. Navy)

(Above) F-4G Phantom of VF-213 recovers aboard USS Kitty Hawk (CVA-63) after a 1965 mission over North Vietnam. Only 12 F-4B Phantoms were modified to F-4G configuration with the addition of ASW-21 tactical communications system. All served with VF-213.

VA-85 was the second A-6A squadron to see combat, flying from the USS Kitty Hawk from November of 1965. The effectiveness of the A-6's all-weather capability was demonstrated by the North Vietnamese charges that the Uong Bi power plant had been struck by B-52s, when in fact, the job had been done by a pair of VA-85 Intruders under cover of night and weather.

(Below) Phantom of VF-151 preparing for launch from Coral Sea for a ground pounding mission.

F-105s of PACAF's 36th TFS were adorned with red ailerons and red arrows on the intakes during their early war efforts from Thailand in 1964. (Dave Graben)

Lt. Dave Graben about to mount his 36th TFS Thud prior to 1964 mission to the Laotian Plain of Jars. The 36th operated from Takhli AB, Thailand.

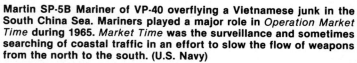

Martin SP-5B Mariner of VP-40 overflying a Vietnamese junk in the South China Sea. Mariners played a major role in *Operation Market Time* during 1965. *Market Time* was the surveillance and sometimes searching of coastal traffic in an effort to slow the flow of weapons from the north to the south. (U.S. Navy)

4th TFW Thud launching a volley of 2.75 inch rockets at a North Vietnamese AAA site on a 1966 mission against the North. Early in the *Rolling Thunder* phase of the air war the F-105 established itself as the prime air to ground weapon in the USAF inventory. It would eventually shoulder 75% of the burden of strikes against the North. (USAF)

Thud lifting off for one of the first strikes against North Vietnam in 1965. It is armed with 750 pound bombs on the centerline MER and rocket pods on the outboard wing pylons. As the anti-aircraft defenses over North Vietnam improved, the 105s began to carry ECM pods and/or Sidewinder AAMs on the outboard pylons. (USAF)

(Left) On the tanker enroute to targets in North Vietnam. Tail bands are from top to bottom: Blue, yellow, red. PACAF badge on tail.

(Below, Left) USAF F-4C in pre-war gull grey paint on the tanker enroute to North Vietnam on an early *Rolling Thunder* mission.

(Below) The F-104C was deployed to Southeast Asia to act in the Combat Air Patrol air defense role. With it's limited range it was not able to accompany the strike forces into North Vietnam, and was eventually employed in the light strike role in the South for a time.

The buildup of U.S. airpower in South Vietnam is graphically illustrated by this December, 1965 photo of the departure end of the runway at Bien Hoa. Civil contract carriers were delivering cargo and troops to the war zone, while fighters and gunships were flying close support missions practically in the landing pattern! (USAF)

Helio U-10B Super Courier was widely used as a courier and liason aircraft, since it's short field capability made it perfect for getting into and out of improvised airstrips. (USAF)

TF-102 was used as a photo chase plane for a B-52 *Arc Light* strike against Viet Cong stronghold 18 miles north of Saigon in December, 1965. (USAF)

(Above) Loading 750LB bombs on F-100D Super Sabre at Bien Hoa, 1965. What the F-105 was to the air war over North Vietnam, the F-100 was to the *In-country* war. Bands on tail are light blue, bomb mission markings on nose are red. (USAF)

F-100D of the 481st TFS rolls in to make a strafing pass in the Mekong Delta, a strike camera is mounted on centerline. The 481st deployed to Tan Son Nhut AB in June, 1965 for a three month combat tour that lasted five months and over 5,000 combat hours, during which they claimed over 1.700 VC, killed, destroyed 3,337 buildings, sunk 147 sampans, and destroyed 11 bunkers, 7 gun emplacements and 3 fuel dumps. (USAF)

One of the early AC-47s carried the name *Grunt 2*, a reference to it's aggressive mission.

The AC-47 was dubbed *Puff the Magic Dragon*, and most used the call sign "Spooky". Their three General Electric Miniguns were each capable of firing 6,000 rounds per minute of 7.62MM ammunition. (USAF)

RB-66's of the 363rd TRW on the flight line at Tan Son Nhut AB in 1965. In addition to reconnaissance duties, the RB-66 was used as a navigational pathfinder for bombers over North Vietnam in the early phases of *Rolling Thunder*. The Destroyer would lead a flight of 105s which flew two on each wing, dropping their bombs on command from the RB-66. Since it had no defensive capability, the RB-66 had to have fighter escort on these missions. (USAF)

Lockheed EC-121 was originally sent to Southeast Asia to monitor the movements of the IL-28 light bombers of North Vietnam, and to provide early warning should they be sent to attack South Vietnam. This radar surveillance mission eventually led to it's use as an airborne controller, providing information to strike flights on Mig movements and navigational information. It's call sign was "College Eye". (USAF)

RF-101s at Tan Son Nhut in 1965. As the missions became more hazardous, camouflage was recognized as a necessity. The Voodoo in the foreground still carried an early, experimental version of camouflage. RF-101s bore the brunt of the reconnaissance duties throughout the early to mid 1960s, beginning with flights over Laos in 1961, and continuing into the heaviest of Rolling Thunder pre and post mission target assessment. (USAF)

(Above) In spite of the popular media portrayal of Americans as indiscriminate killers, there were innumerable examples of the finest of American traits. Sgt. Pedro Corral, of the 309th Air Commando Squadron at Tan Son Nhut, distributed Christmas presents to Vietnamese children in 1965.

(Above Left) Marine CH-46A about to relocate Vietnamese civilians from one of the more hotly contested areas in the Northern provinces.

(Left) Skyraiders of the VNAF strafe Viet Cong troops along a canal near Than Minh in 1965. One of the first actions taken by Nguyen Cao Ky upon his appointment to head the VNAF was to request replacement of the T-28 with the more potent A-1. Transition training often took place in combat, with members of the Air Commandos flying as instructors to VNAF pilots. (USAF)

(Below) Battle damaged A-1E returning to Bien Hoa after a 1965 combat mission. The 602nd Fighter Squadron (Commando) was formed at Bien Hoa in 1964 as the first USAF Skyraider unit in the country. (USAF)

Loading 500LB bombs on an A-1E at Bien Hoa. The 1st Air Commando Squadron turned in their tired T-28Ds in 1964, switching to the Spad. With it's fantastic load-carrying capability (8,000LBS of external ord-nance), great endurance (out to 3,000 miles), and ability to absorb punishment, the A-1 became one of the premier performers in the close air support and RESCAP roles, serving until the end of the war. (Right) Sgt. William Russell of the 34th Tactical Group at Bien Hoa is fusing a 260LB bomb on an A-1E, while Captain Charles C. Vasiliadis (Below) preflights his Skyraider, which is loaded with 500LB "Daisy Cutters". This bomb configuration was first introduced in World War II, and assured that the bomb would burst above ground. (USAF)

(Below) A-1E of the 1st Air Commandos taxies in post-mission, Bien Hoa, 1965.

A-1Es taxi to their revetments after a training mission/strike against the Viet Cong. The two place A-1E was used extensively to transition VNAF pilots to their new fighter-bomber. (USAF)

The Spad was used to support U.S. Special Forces camps, which were often placed in precarious positions in order to draw the enemy out. When attacked, they needed quick and effective air support. The A-1 was often able to get in under weather that frustrated the fast movers. On one such mission, in support of the Special Forces camp at A Shau, Major Bernie Fisher won the Medal of Honor for landing his Skyraider on the debris strewn and damaged PSP strip to rescue a shot-down fellow pilot. That action took place on March 10, 1966. (USAF)

The CH-46 entered combat in March, 1966, with the arrival of 27 machines of HMM-164. They were joined in June by HMM-265. Both squadrons operated from Marble Mountain, near Danang. (USMC)

(Below) The TF-9J Panther was used by the Marines as an airborne tactical air coordinator. They were based at Danang. (via John Santucci)

(Below) The EF-10B was used in the Electronic Warfare role, providing threat identification for the B-57 night bombers, as well as it's regular duties with the Marines. (via John Santucci)

VMFA-531 was the first Marine Fighter Squadron to deploy the F-4 Phantom to Vietnam, arriving at Danang on 11 April, 1965 from Atsugi, Japan. They were refueled enroute by Marine KC-130 tankers. They flew their first combat missions the following day. (USMC)

F-8E of VMF (AW) 232. The Red Devils was the third F-8 Marine Squadron to arrive in Vietnam, beginning operations from Danang in December, 1966.

B-52s began flying tactical air strikes against Viet Cong strongholds throughout South Vietnam in 1965. The first strike was flown 18 June, 1965. Unfortunately, two of the B-52s had a mid-air collision during in-flight refueling and 8 of the 12 crewmen died as both crashed into the ocean. (USAF)

(Above) *Lady Luck* was the first and only B-52F to fly more than 100 combat missions. It was assigned to the 454th Bomb Wing, 736th Bomb Squadron, Andersen AFB, Guam. (Charles B. Mayer)

(Above) *Mekong Express*, a B-52F was also assigned to the 454th. Introduction of the B-52 to the war created a furor in the media, but it quickly proved to be a very accurate and effective weapon. *Arc Light* strikes were flown from altitudes of 20,000 to 30,000 feet. Often the Viet Cong had no idea that they were under attack until long strings of bombs began marching across the jungles. (Charles B. Mayer)

(Right) F-102s were still providing air defense for Tan Son Nhut early in 1966. (USAF)

A-6A of VA-75, flown by Captain (then Lt.) Don Boecker inbound to target in North Vietnam. The A-6 proved the value of it's radar bombing system in it's first combat deployment in 1965, flying in the worst weather, at night whenever possible.

A-6A of VA-65 catches the number two wire in this September, 1966, trap aboard Constellation after a mission over North Vietnam. The two tone green camouflage was applied on a trial basis to the A-6s of VA-65 and VA-85, but was not adopted. (U.S. Navy)

Ordnancemen wear red aboard carriers. In this 1966 shot they are loading an A-6A of VA-85 for a mission against North Vietnam from U.S.S. Kitty Hawk. (U.S. Navy)

Naval Aviator heads for his aircraft prior to a combat mission over North Vietnam. (U.S. Navy)

(Above) The CH-37 Mojave provided heavy lift capabilities for the U.S. Army early in the U.S. buildup. (U.S. Army)

(Below) UH-1D Hueys of the 1st Bn, 7th Cav Regt, 1st Cav Div (Airmobile) landing at An Khe during an air assault in December, 1965.

Base defense was a problem in the Vietnam War from the outset, and the USAF employed sentry dogs to augment it's perimeter defenses. Here they pass in review at Tan Son Nhut, April, 1966. (USAF)

(Above) Lockheed C-140 Jet Star was used for intra-theater courier and VIP transport duties. Tan Son Nhut, December, 1966. (USAF)

Base defenses suffered when the base was jointly operated by USAF and VNAF because of the difficulties involved in coordinating defenses outside of the perimeter. The proximity of most bases to either urban or dense jungle areas (both ideal cover for infiltrators) complicated this. Naturally, night was the time of maximum danger, and in times when attack was deemed most likely, flares kept the night alive. The best defenses were those fully coordinated with the ground commanders, such as at Army bases or at Danang, which had the best overall defense of any of the large airbases. (USAF)

Lockheed P-2 Neptune was used to patrol the Vietnamese coast in search of contraband carrying Junks, in Operation Market Time.

F-8E of VMF (AW) 235, as it appeared at DaNang RVN, 1966.

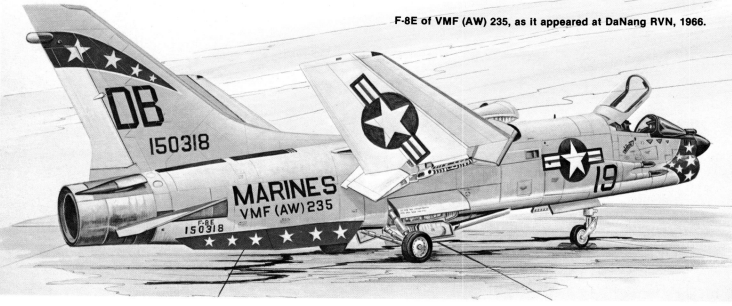

The Marines used the TF-9J for armed reconnaissance from Danang in 1966. This shark-mouth was assigned to MAG-11.

Grumman HU-16B was used by USAF for Gulf of Tonkin rescues of downed pilots. This aircraft was based at Danang in 1966.

F-100s of the 7th Air Force at Osan AB, ROK, 1963. (Richard Copsey)

F-105s flying from bases in Thailand saw combat action against the Pathet Lao in the Plain of Jars, Laos, in 1964.

The first Phantoms to fight in Vietnam went into combat in their "peacetime" clothes of grey over white.

(Above) While the F-105 was famous for the large role it played in the air war against North Vietnam, it was not restricted to the north. These Thuds are loaded for a *Skyspot* bombing mission in South Vietnam. The *Skyspot* system originated as a method of electronically scoring simulated bomb drops by triangulation. It proved equally effective as a method of bombing through a solid overcast. (USAF)

F-105s flew often and their missions were among the toughest in the war, requiring the constant attention of the ground crews. The big J-75 engine gave the Thud it's high rate of knots on the deck, and the pilots used that speed on every mission. Engines were changed often. (Republic)

By 1966, the pattern of the air war against North Vietnam had been established, with the bulk of USAF strikes coming from six airfields in Thailand. USAF strength in Thailand rising from 1,000 personnel and 83 aircraft in 1965 to 35,000 personnel and over 600 aircraft by 1968. The F-105 carried out 75% of the strikes against the north, and many of the heroes of the Vietnam War were F-105 pilots. 1st Lts Fred Wilson and Karl Richter got two of the 25 Migs eventually credited to the Thud. Richter was the youngest Mig killer of the war at that time. Richter was also the high combat time 105 pilot at the time of his death, on his 198th combat mission. He is at right in the photo at right. The practice of naming aircraft was revived in Vietnam and the popular literary hero of the day was James Bond, AKA *007*. F-105 of the 388th TFW on it's takeoff roll from Korat RTAB, 1966. (USAF)

A-1H of VA-52 was CAG aircraft of air wing 19, aboard Ticonderoga, 1966.

UH-1B with M-6 machine gun system and rockets as it appeared in 1964 support mission.

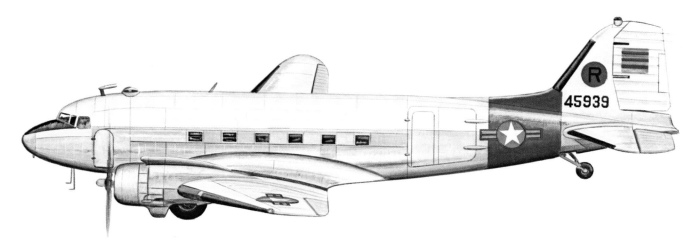

C-47 flown by American pilots in support of the Vietnamese in 1962 was turned over to the VNAF in 1963 when enough Vietnamese pilots had been trained to operate the C-47.

T-28C of the 1st Air Commando Squadron, flown by USAF and South Vietnamese crews out of Bien Hoa and Soc Trang, 1963-64.

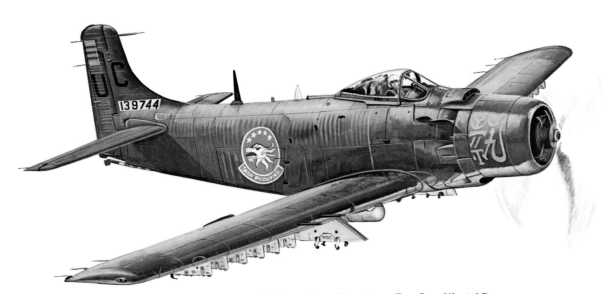

A-1H of the 83rd Special Operations Squadron, Tan Son Nhut AB. This unit was commanded by Nguyen Cao Ky, later President of RVN.

The F-5A Freedom Fighter was combat tested by the 4503rd Tactical Fighter Squadron, under the *Skoshi Tiger* program at Bien Hoa AB in October, 1965. The evaluation was concluded four months later. *The F-5s* of the 4503rd were then turned over to the 10th Fighter Commando Squadron, one of which is seen here in June, 1966. (Menard)

F-102 Delta Dagger of the 599th FIS at Bien Hoa AB, November, 1966. The F-102s were often used to escort VIP and civilian flights in "show the flag" air defense flights. (USAF)

Capt. Mark Anderson and Lt. Robert Pollock of the 510th TFS revive another World War II tradition by sending explosive birthday greetings to Ho Chi Minh, Bien Hoa, May 1966. (USAF)

Project *Charging Sparrow* was a USAF directed program designed to test the reliability of the AIM-7 missile, after having been subjected to the rigors of Southeast Asian weather and combat missions. F-4Cs from Cam Rahn Bay left Vietnam on 12 December, 1966, flew to Clark AB in the Phillipines, were briefed, then fired their missiles in missions the following day, and flew back to Cam Ranh Bay. (USAF)

The F-4D began operations in 1966, at the same time that a furor erupted over a "bomb shortage". It had become obvious to some commanders that the people in Washington were determining the success of the war effort according to the number of sorties flown. While there were some interruptions in munitions supply, they were accentuated by flying aircraft with less than full loads in order to roll up the number of sorties. (USAF)

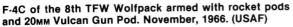

F-4C of the 8th TFW Wolfpack armed with rocket pods and 20MM Vulcan Gun Pod. November, 1966. (USAF)

UH-34 of Marine Medium Helicopter Squadron 361 as it appeared in 1963, while used in support of ARVN operations. HMM-361 lost 12 KIA and 19 wounded, while having three of their UH-34's shot down in late 1963.

B-57s of the 8th and 13th Bomb Squadrons at Bien Hoa AB, RVN, 1964. After the disastrous Viet Cong attack of November 1, lineups such as this became rare, as planes were dispersed to blast-protective revetments. (USAF)

F-86s of the Royal Australian Air Force flew from Takhli RTAB. They were used as base air defense. (Don Kutyna)

The CIAs airline, Air America, used a wide variety of aircraft in its operations throughout Southeast Asia, including this C-46, photographed at Osan AB, ROK in 1963. (Richard Copsey)

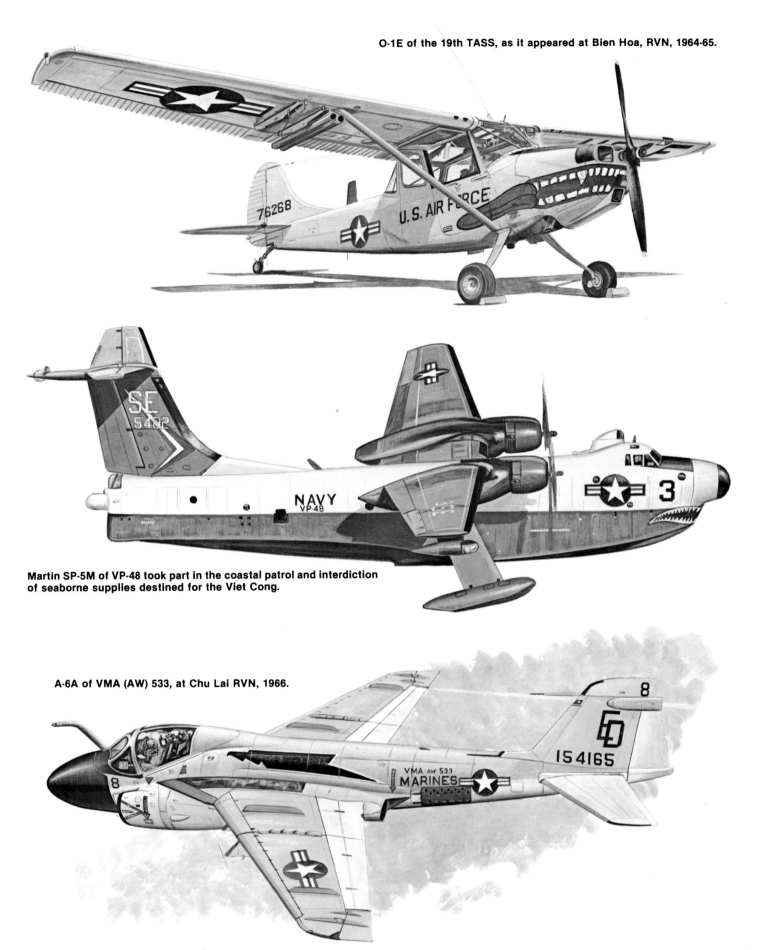

O-1E of the 19th TASS, as it appeared at Bien Hoa, RVN, 1964-65.

Martin SP-5M of VP-48 took part in the coastal patrol and interdiction of seaborne supplies destined for the Viet Cong.

A-6A of VMA (AW) 533, at Chu Lai RVN, 1966.

After several engagements with Mig-17s, in which an experienced American pilot might be able to manuever into the 6 O-Clock of the Mig, but be inside of minimum range for it's missiles, some F-4s began to carry the Vulcan Gun Pod on the centerline. (USAF)

Fighter Pilots will always talk with their hands, and Vietnam was no exception. Max Cameron demonstrates how he shot down a Mig-17 in April, 1966. (USAF)

Typical SAM site in North Vietnam. (USAF)

750 pound bomb being loaded on an F-4C at Ubon RTAB. (USAF)

Major Paul Gilmore (left) and his GIB, 1st Lt. William T. Smith, were the first to shoot down a Mig-21, scoring the kill on April 26, 1966. (USAF)

Mig-17s at Phuc Yen in October, 1966. (USAF)

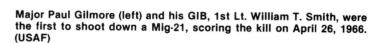

A-1E Skyraiders began escorting the rescue forces in August, 1965, a role which they would play until the end of the war. The Spad above is armed with the 7.62MM minigun pod. In addition to providing suppressive fire for the rescue helicopters, the A-1s usually preceded the helo into the rescue area to locate the downed pilots. (USAF)

The pilot of the AC-47 could devastate a given area with his three 6,000 rounds-per-minute miniguns. (USAF)

Bell Aerosystems/Navy PACV (SK-5) was based at Cat Lo, near Vung Tau from May, 1966 and was used in Operation Market Time.

F-4B of VMFA-115 at Danang, late 1966. (USMC)

At the beginning of the Vietnam War the only dedicated Air Rescue helicopter in the USAF inventory was the HH-43. It's primary job in the United States had been fire-suppression and rescue on the air base. Conditions in Southeast Asia required the Huskie to perform in that and many other roles, such as recovery of the wounded or downed aircrew from the combat zone. That it was able to perform this role until the introduction of the CH-3 is a tribute to it's pedigree and to it's crews. Both of the aircraft seen were assigned to Detachment 4, Pacific Air Rescue Center, and operated from Bien Hoa in 1964-65. (USAF)

Helio U-10B Courier at Danang, January, 1966. (USAF)

Helio U-10B was used in a variety of missions, one of which was the distribution of psychological warfare leaflets such as the one at left, which is a safe-conduct pass guaranteeing fair treatment to any VC who surrendered. (USAF and Norman Taylor)

(Below Left) USAF 1st Lt. Alex Zakrzeski had won 3 DFC's, 11 Air Medals, and six Vietnamese awards while flying the O-1 as a FAC when this picture was taken in 1966. (USAF)

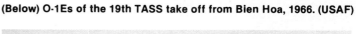

(Below) O-1Es of the 19th TASS take off from Bien Hoa, 1966. (USAF)

(Above) C-123 of *Operation Ranch Hand* spraying defoliants on the Vietnamese jungle in 1966. The now-infamous Agent Orange was used to deny VC the cover and concealment of the triple canopy rain forests. Ranch Hand was one of the more dangerous missions, requiring the 123s to fly low and slow over what were presumed to be verified enemy areas. They were often shot at, even though escorted by some sort of a fighter that could retaliate. (USAF)

(Above) The versatility of the C-123 and the professionalism of it's crews were graphically demonstrated during *Operation Attleboro*, November 6, 1966. This 30 foot wide strip at Dau Tieng saw a landing every 7 minutes during one four hour period. (USAF)

By mid-1966 the newly arrived CH-3s were flying not only rescue missions, but also heavy lift assignments for the Vietnamese. (USAF)

A portion of Bien Hoa Air Base as it appeared in January, 1966. The large parking ramps would soon be subdivided and filled with blast deflectors and American aircraft. (USAF)

The UH-34 was the first Marine helicopter assigned to Vietnam, and remained as one of the most important throughout the 1960s, in spite of official plans to retire it sooner. It is seen here disembarking combat troops on Foxtrot Ridge. (USMC)

Marines board a CH-46 Sea Knight prior to hitting the beach. Aboard the USS Princeton (LPH-5), April, 1966. (USMC)

CH-46A of HMM-164 at Danang, May, 1966. As they gained time in the combat zone, the 46s lost their high-visibility markings, and glossy clean finishes. (USMC)

F-4B of VMFA-115 on a close support mission in April, 1966. (USMC)

(Above) The same F-4 begins its roll-in to drop Snakeye bombs. Marines used the Phantom almost exclusively in the close-support role. (USMC)

A pair of VMFA-542 Phantoms enroute to targets in Northern I Corps. They are armed with Snakeye high-drag bombs and rocket pods. The absence of any air-to-air weaponry is significant only in that it was normal. (USMC)

(Above and Below) Another great air-to-air fighter which the Marines used almost exclusively to move mud was the F-8 Crusader. VMF (AW) 235 *Death Angels* operated their F-8Es from Danang in 1966. A favored weapons load was Zuni rocket pods on the fuselage hard points normally used for Sidewinder AAM's. (John Santucci and USMC)

Result of a Viet Cong sapper attack at Danang in 1966. Though Danang had the best overall base defenses, it's proximity to one of the consistently hottest areas of the war zone made it a regular target for enemy infiltrators and rocket attacks.

A portable crane hoisting high drag bombs to be loaded on a Skyhawk of VMA-214 at Chu Lai. September, 1966. (USMC)

A-4E of VMA-214 at Chu Lai, May, 1966. It is armed with a pair of napalm bombs. The Skyhawk was one of the most consistant performers of the Vietnam War, and served with the Marines from the beginning until the end. (USMC)

A-6A of VMA (AW) 242 enroute to target with 500LB "slick" bombs. 242 operated from Danang, as a part of MAG-11. Marine A-6s flew missions against North Vietnam as well as the traditional pure support role for the Marine Grunt. (USMC)

Most Marine A-6 strikes against the north were flown at night, and they ranged as far north as Hanoi with EA-6s providing jamming of AAA and SAM sites and F-4s flying MIGCAP. (USMC)

EA-6A of VMCJ-1 at Danang, late 1966. The EA-6A made its combat debut in November, 1966. It was used primarily as an Electronics Countermeasures aircraft, but also performed reconnaissance, escort for B-52s, and support for tactical air strikes. It replaced the EF-10B. (USMC)

A-6A of VMA (AW) 225 being armed at Danang. (USMC)

F-4Bs from VF-92 enroute to targets in South Vietnam, while flying off the USS Enterprise on Dixie Station. Early in the war, a "warmup" period was given to newly arriving carrier air wings. They flew missions from Dixie Station, into the relatively light air-defense environment of South Vietnam, before moving to the big leagues...Yankee Station, off the coast of North Vietnam. (U.S. Navy)

Dumping fuel to get down to landing weight on return to the carrier. (U.S. Navy)

Coming aboard after a strike. The LSO is able to give the pilot advice as he makes his approach, aiming for the number three wire. The F-4 proved to be one of the easiest landing fighters. (If that is not a contradiction in terms.) (U.S. Navy)

USS Hancock (CVA-19) readying for the launch of Air Group 21 for strikes against Viet Cong positions in South Vietnam, June, 1966. (U.S. Navy)

USS Oriskany (CVA-34) launching an F-8E of VF-162 for a mission against North Vietnam, July, 1966, Air Group 16, with VF-111, VF-162, VA-162, VA-163, VA-164, VAH-4, VAW-12 and VFP-63 were aboard during this cruise. (U.S. Navy)

Two views of operations on the deck of the Nuclear Carrier USS Enterprise CVAN-65 in the spring of 1966. Green camouflage was tried on a number of navy aircraft, from several carriers in 1965-66. It was judged to be more of a hazard to deck crews during night operations than the limited (and questionable) protection it afforded it's pilots. It's use was discontinued in late 1966. (U.S. Navy)

(Above) F-4Bs of VF-161 being refuelled by a KA-3B of VAH-8 after a September 1966 strike against North Vietnam. (U.S. Navy)

A-4Cs of VA-113 prior to launch from the USS Enterprise for a strike against North Vietnam. Air Group 9s cruise aboard Enterprise began in December, 1966. (U.S. Navy)

(Above) F-4B of VF-92 straining against holdback cables prior to launch from Enterprise. Vital launch weight information is recorded in chalk on the side of the cooling air intake. (U.S. Navy)

USS Coral Sea (CVA-43) Air Group 15 carried out some of the *Flaming Dart* strikes against North Vietnam in February, 1965, and received the first Navy Unit Commendation of the Vietnam War. (U.S. Navy)

F-4Bs of VF-96 enroute to targets in North Vietnam, 1966. (U.S. Navy)

(Above) USS Franklin D. Roosevelt (CVA-42) carried Air Group 1, which consisted of VF-11, VF-14, VA-12, VA-172, VAH-10, VAW-12, VQ-2 and VFP-62 into combat in 1966. (U.S. Navy)

(Below) USS Constellation (CVA-64) carried Air Group 15 in 1966. VF-151, VF-161, VA-65, VA-153, VA-155, RVAH-6, VAH-8 and VAW-11. (U.S. Navy)

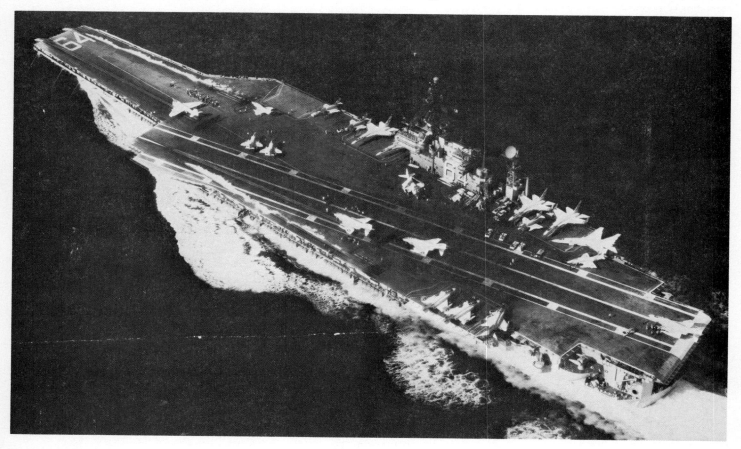

VA-85 was the second squadron to take the Intruder into combat, following VA-75, which had given the A-6 its baptism of fire in 1965. (U.S. Navy)

(Below) VA-85 Intruders ready for a mission against the north, April, 1966.

(Bottom) Upraised arms of deck edge catapult operator signifies that the system is ready for operation. USS Kitty Hawk, Gulf of Tonkin, April, 1966.

KA-3B "Whale" with it's refuelling hose and basket deployed for the use of the A-6 from which the picture was taken. Though it was orginally designed as a heavy attack bomber, the A-3 proved most useful in the aerial tanker role. (U.S. Navy)

F-4B Phantom II about to catch the wire aboard USS Kitty Hawk after a 1966 strike. (U.S. Navy)

(Above) RF-8G of VFP-63 took a hit over North Vietnam, but managed to make it back to Danang. It was part of the detachment aboard USS Bon Homme Richard embarked with Air Group 19 in 1966. (Neal Schnieder)

F-8E of VF-111 generating tip vortice contrails in a high-G pullout after bomb release. (U.S. Navy)

(Above) Commander Dick Bellinger, CO of VF-162 climbs down from his Crusader after a mission over the north. (U.S. Navy)

(Left) North Vietnamese oil lighter burning after being hit by attack aircraft from the USS Constellation in October, 1966. The procrastination of the Johnson Administration when it came to hitting POL stocks allowed the North Vietnamese to disperse the majority of their supplies. Hits such as this were all too few and far between. (U.S. Navy)

(Below) F-8 of VF-51 firing a Zuni rocket at a Viet Cong position in South Vietnam, 1966. (U.S. Navy)

(Above) VA-12 Skyhawk completes a trap aboard USS Franklin D. Roosevelt after a 10 August, 1966 strike against North Vietnam. (U.S. Navy)

(Above) Commander Hal Marr, C.O. of VF-211, was the first F-8 pilot to shoot down a Mig, knocking down the Mig-17 on 12 June, 1966. *Beautimus* is being attached to the catapult aboard Hancock, April 6, 1966, in preparation for a strike against the North. (U.S. Navy)

Tooter Teague's F-8 swallows the crew chief during the postflight check after a mission against the North in September, 1966. (U.S. Navy)

(Above) The Catapult Officer aboard Oriskany signals for the launch of an F-8 of VF-111 *Sundowners* on 12 October, 1966, during SECDEF McNamara's tour. (U.S. Navy)

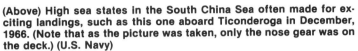

(Below) Lowest of the low-level air war was fought by Patrol Air Cushion Vehicles, who never got more than a few inches off the surface. They were used extensively in *Market Time* operations, stopping and searching coastal traffic in an effort to impede the flow of arms from North Vietnam. (U.S. Navy)

(Above) High sea states in the South China Sea often made for exciting landings, such as this one aboard Ticonderoga in December, 1966. (Note that as the picture was taken, only the nose gear was on the deck.) (U.S. Navy)

(Above) Also used in *Operation Market Time* was the SP2H Neptune, seen here patrolling the coast south of Vung Tau. (U.S. Navy)

(Below) A-1H of VA-152 lightly loaded for a mission over Vietnam during the 1965 Oriskany cruise of Air Group 16.

(Below) VA-115 *Arabs* A-1H inbound to North Vietnam, under the radar, 1966. (U.S. Navy)

Parochial infighting eventually led to transfer of all Army Caribous to USAF, which was adamant in it's insistence that only the Air Force could handle coordination of all fixed-wing airlift assets. The Army was still flying CV-2s when this picture was taken in 1966. (USAF)

The OV-1 Mohawk served with the US Army from 1962 as a reconnaissance aircraft which could provide photographic coverage of suspected enemy areas. The Mohawk was unsurpassed in the speed at which such intelligence could be diseminated to field commanders. (U.S. Army)

Many of the Army's civic action programs included transportation of Vietnamese civilians from areas targeted for search and destroy missions. The Boeing Vertol CH-47 Chinook was the Army's most widely used heavy hauler. (U.S. Army)

Chinook unloads a 2½ ton truck at the 1st Infantry Division's Heliport at DI-AN, South Vietnam, February, 1966. (U.S. Army)

CH-54 Flying Crane was used for the really heavy lifting jobs in Vietnam, including salvage of this F-4B of VF-154, which made a forced landing at Danang after suffering battle damage over the North. October, 1966. (U.S. Army)

The UH-1B Huey became the primary armed helicopter during the early phases of the Vietnam War. It is shown here in two versions. At left and below, with the XM-31 20MM cannon as flown by the 145th Aviation Battalion from Bien Hoa in April, 1966. Above, it is armed with rockets and the M-6 flexible quad 30 caliber machine guns. (U.S. Army)

(Above) This is a scene that perhaps more than any other, will evoke the aura of the Vietnam War. It became the first war in which Airmobility was a decisive factor. UH-1D "Slicks" have offloaded troops in a rice paddy during an assault mission in the Bong Son, January, 1966. (U.S. Army)

SP/4 Bobby R. Hamby, gunner with the *Joker* Platoon, 48th Assault Helicopter Company, 10th Aviation Bn, checks the sighting and trigger mechanism of the XM-16 Armament System aboard a UH-1B Huey Hog gunship at Tuy Hoa, September, 1966. (U.S. Army)

(Above) Hueys of the 13th "Delta" Aviation Battalion carry ARVN troops to an LZ that has been prepped with heavy bombing. (U.S. Army)

(Below) The CH-54 Skycrane could transport this fully mobile battlefield hospital operating theater right to the battlefield. (U.S. Army)

During July of 1966 the 101st Airborne Division participated in *Operation John Paul Jones.* The 2nd Battalion of the 502nd Infantry assaulted Vung Ro Bay Beach, then headed north to link up with the 327th Infantry on Route One. (U.S. Army)

Eagle Flight UH-1 Huey delivering supplies to a Special Forces Camp. (U.S. Army)

The first troops hit the beach at Vung Ro Bay, 24 July, 1966. (U.S. Army)

By the middle of 1966 the mobility afforded by the Helicopter, combined with the ever-increasing weight of American firepower, had made it almost impossible for the communists to win any significant battles. The Huey was the most ubiquitous weapon of the war, serving in all of the allied armed forces, as well as every branch of the American fighting forces, from the Delta in the south, to the DMZ in the north. (U.S. Army)

Because of the mobility the helicopter gave the allies, combat casualties were more likely to receive emergency medical treatment faster than they would have in the United States. (U.S. Army)

Hueys lifting off after lifting troops into an LZ. (Bell)

Army Combat Cameraman operating a 16MM camera from the Nelson Tyler Mount aboard a Huey, during *Operation Deckhouse V*, January, 1967. (U.S. Army)

(Above) Another special mission performed by the Huey was the *Lightning Bug,* a field modification made from the landing lights of a C-130. It was used for night surveillance of Special Forces Camps and base camp perimeters. Ton Son Nhut, February, 1966. (U.S. Army)

The UH-1D was also modified for the *Lightning Bug* mission. Unusual door gun armament is this 50 caliber machine gun. (U.S. Army)

(Above) The T-28 was nearly forgotten when it came to assignment of tactical targets in 1966. It was overshadowed by the bigger and more heavily armed A-1s of the VNAF, and by the increasing numbers of U.S. jets by late 1966. (via Norman E. Taylor)

VNAF A-1H. (Norm Taylor Collection)

Members of the last VNAF class to be trained by U.S. pilots at Bien Hoa. They are shown with the CO of the 602nd Fighter Squadron, Col. Eugene L. Surowiec and Capt. Thomas D. Pullman. The VNAF 522nd Fighter Squadron was stationed at Tan Son Nhut and was under the direct control of Premier Ky. The Chinese character on the nose is based on the ace in a pack of cards. (USAF)

VNAF A-1H at Bien Hoa, 1965. Crater from VC mortar round in foreground. (Norm Taylor Collection)

The 522nd Fighter Squadron later adopted the yellow/black checkboard on it's fuselage. This A-1H was forced to make a wheels-up landing after suffering battle damage in June, 1966. (USAF)

VNAF A-1s at Bien Hoa, 1965. (Norm Taylor Collection)

VNAF C-47 at the Dalat Cam-Ly Airport, with the Passenger Terminal in the background. (Norm Taylor Collection)

The Gooney was among the first aircraft to be operated by the South Vietnamese, who inherited several from the French. With the increase in American involvement, more C-47s were supplied, and U.S. pilots did much of the training. These C-47s are from the 1st Transport Group and were flown by U.S. pilots who were known as the "Dirty Thirty". They had been assigned to fly non-combatant missions, in order to free up experienced VNAF pilots for missions in the T-28 attack fighters. (Norm Taylor Collection)

Royal Thai Air Force F-86Ls join up with a USAF TF-102 over Thailand during a joint training exercise in 1966. Thai Air Force fighters flew air defense missions over their own bases, which were jointly used by USAF fighters and bombers flying missions against North Vietnam. (USAF)

C-47A of the Royal Laotian Air Force at Ubon RTAFB, Thailand. (Albert Piccirillo via Norm Taylor)

C-47A of the Royal Thai Air Force at Ubon. (Al Piccirillo via Norm Taylor)

The H-34 Choctaw was the first helicopter received by the VNAF in quantities sufficient to provide the Vietnamese with an indigenous airlift capability. There were eventually five squadrons, with two at Danang, and one each at Tan Son Nhut, Binh Thuy and Nha Trang. (Norman Taylor Collection)

B-26K Counter Invader became one of the principle weapons in the war against the Ho Chi Minh Trail. This B-26 is armed with anti-personnel weapons. It was assigned to the 609th Special Operations Squadron, 56th Special Operations Group, Nakhon Phanom Royal Thai Air Base. (Norm Taylor Collection)